OUR GRIEVING
EDEN

Marc Williams

Copyright © 2011 Mr. Marc Lee Williams
All rights reserved.

ISBN: 1463553641
ISBN-13: 9781463553647

for Karen,

who blessedly stays

TABLE OF CONTENTS

I   Our Cocoon Less Bruised   vii

After Love Became Our Grieving Eden   1

Our Fermenting Sourness   4

Blaming Tastes Of Showdown   7

Our Ivy-Choked Sin Creeping Skyward   9

Our Cocoon Less Bruised   12

Our Middling Age   14

Our Silver Anniversary, Heart-Fully Untarnished   16

Whose Love Lifely Conscripted   19

Before You Leave   22

II   Not Yet, Go Back   **25**

At The Bottom Of My Well   27

Myth Writhing Into Life   30

Creaky & Leaking   33

Muscular Knots of Poverty   36

Accordian Steps   39

After The War   42

Our 4,000 Soldiers Patroling Heaven   46

Before The Political	49
Our Last American Manifesto	51
What Every Torture Memo Says	55
An Earned Servant Speaketh	59
This Daily Soliloquy	62
This Yuletide's Tongue Speaking Freely	68
Banish Us Outward	73

I

Our Cocoon Less Bruised

AFTER LOVE BECAME OUR GRIEVING EDEN

I always marry the wrong man
dreamt at least weekly after hours
of wakeful pacing all over the bed
to be relieved of a(nother) husband
who surely crossed his fingers at the altar
once the vows steadily questioned our intent
to love one another forever in joy & trouble,

whatever I knew of you before our wedding day
became squashed by the damage afterward,
it is the kissing risk of matrimony to shroud
our senses with love's prized lightning
scenting our lives until the later that quakes
faster than any burial can happen. Love
tickles & infects us,it strokes our faces,
wipes our tears,fondles us & strangles us
in our sleep,it demands that we leap higher
than Providence can guarantee its benefact,
its arcane murmurings burn our yearning ears
& constipate our hearts,yet the next man
must be given your chance,since,if all men
are the same,you speak such a cock'd language
understood only by yourselves.
                                            The wrong man
is knifishly hurt-full,is selfishly proud
& never whispers that love curdles your heart,

you spend your time near me not bothering
to talk but yelling if perturbed at all
until I serve your distemper as one hired
by the wealthy to mend what your break
        in betrothed,churning bondage
        to an ancient notion of maleness
called *adore me as a man-god who walks
well upon the earth*—-some wrong men
throw water in my face or spit in my ears,
some drink until you slur your burly rage
while others slap me with your manly bruises

as the oozing proof women can always be hard-won
& the cheating ones creep quietly behind me
to commit your sillier sin of fucking others
because I have failed you as the man halo'd
from the aura of your resplendence. I rarely leave
this pinched territory of masculine customs
to splay myself on the floor of my own house
because my heart blocks me at the doorway

to remember love runs as the gauging necessity
in my veins, swirling within its hues & perfume
no infinite wisdom but what other touchable air
that thrives a lifetime in me. I have lived
all these maladies before in childhood
's blurry purgatory: a mother who suffered
at the hands of my daily wayward father,

who piled all the vices upon his shoulders
& christened me early with ever-fresh turmoil
sprinkled in my hair well before bedtime—-
if even the right man is no teddy-bear,
then where safely ranges my stomach'd love
            for the breadth & depth of me,
how does my gullible heart anneal its youth
to deflect the lies & lacerations of deathly men?
Who tacitly lets a young woman live alone
before romping hard with a man, children
sooner than maturity's steadfast soul-grip,
when does my trembling about righting you
either cease or rile me to straighten you
or to leave, how does a woman fight a man
with our unmuscled sentiment?
                            What clots
in every woman easing ourselves altogether
from the clutches of any arrogant man

is to nudge our deserved courage into the muddy vortex
          between our sappy hearts & whirling minds
to kiln our gooey love into a soul-stone
          of blessed favour day after year;

how you must treat us scratched in taut prose
on our forearms to remind us at dawn & dusk
there must be hints of worship in your manner
even before the altar—-let our senses answer
this situ'd brutal question about any man
's fondness for women: can we ride atop you
nearly all the time? Who (ab)uses our influence
to push & pull each other toward the tonic
of a marriage,its home-chord in harmony
's wedded scales chiming or clashing every day,
who circles whom or who gallops off elsewhere
once the knotty friction comes—-I grow puissant
-ly charged to shelter myself first,to sacrifice you
when necessary,so place me on a pedestal no higher
than the worst goddess who fatally shames men,
call me home whenever the yoke between us
gets stretched & frayed,never strike me with slaps
or fists in the cheap pummeling of the fairer-—
I need for a man to cover me with yourself
warmer than blandness,looser than jealousy
& pricklier than bad romance novels,I needing
a man who immures me with only lasting up-raise.

June 6-9, 2005

OUR FERMENTING SOURNESS

Wrestling amidst all the miasmic damage
before & since what infection divorce inflicts
from the bloody tongues of you blue accusers
heaving with the stamina of perennial contestants
for Saturday morning television, you plop down
in my office to offer your seething scuttlebutt
about each other in the matter of your children,
whose parenting could be construed as sad wastage
were your vitriol mere candy. If I only listened
to each of you intently & left my heart at home
I would feel like your rattle-minded little kids,
who cry & cling to your legs when one of you
leaves the house to pick them (back) up again
        such is the labour of visitation,
four elements in the bent weather of a human tornado
swirling thru the house that once corralled you
& witnessed some such curdled love. My mind
wanders to scenes of your love exploring itself
before the distemper & collapse, before any others
& before your hands only circling each other
            in a bad-music'd razor-dance
--at the end of each of these exhausting hours
I want to place only the two of you on an island
with a single cell phone with its dying battery
to bet on whether love or rage bleeds thru you,
how implacably crazy is a crumbled marriage
displayed for our gawking & unweeping dis-ease.

      *

HE: You were the younger woman singular enough
to lure me upon the altar, a sultry brunette
temptress whose breasts first fingered me
from afar until I beastly closed the distance
& caressed your face with my soft smiles,
it was raggeder on thru our courtship
but marriage demands strong testimony
of love's pricklier hardship & we obliged
until the stammering lasted too long to love you

well before forever. Maybe the kids clubbed
your disposition with their puerile body-sucking
as how such young ones devour their mother,
but I found the mistress that is my work
past quitting time, your breasts belonging to them
before I came to bed to be teased then scorned.
Children are the crack-less mirrors we fancy
once grown-ups show ourselves ruder than foolish,
both upon your lap at once when the world is
beautifully full, I took snapshots with no camera
while whispering congratulations. I never saw
the cliff coming when I came home early
to find you fucking him with his stinger-cock
doggy-style & yelping as I had never so
gifted you, not only heart-broken women
scream for the black orgasm of divorce—-
I left with my pants down around my ankles
with my belongings piled on top of my head
as do African women carrying home new purchases
to be sold by trade, women still startling men
by jerking our heads toward your favour.

SHE: What oozed from you once the kids
were born was some misguided mourning
of me the fondlable sex-wife lost upon
motherhood's daily work to raise them
as a housed wife who had once worked
but sacrificed my career to ground them
in the giggly pageantry of minded play-time,
you could not romp on the floor & sing
their silly songs or even help with the house-work
if I was tired—-spend your day with kids
crawling all over you & soon silence writhes
in your belly to be healed with nothing
more burdensome: *do a little of what I do
every day, your children are our keep-sakes,
what of them whispers to you at bed-time
to render them so special?* Could our kids
have grown you taller than your heart
's short-sighted love of where we went
          as a family of bettered strength,
what shall be your legacy beyond court cases
& distant verdicts? What abrades a woman
's heart about a man is to feel loosened

on the wandering walk from the altar to the grave,
step for step,thru thunder or down-pouring light--
how our children force us to attend to them
in twining ourselves to haul their upbringing
upon our shoulders,so how often did you delve
into their lives to upright them?
                                    You caught me
with a better father,I know of his talents
& he heard about your malaise,his penis
no larger than his heart,if such wreckage
I coarsely caused what did you lack beforehand,
what kept you hobbling behind me as a stray waif?

              *   *

I breathe both your hearts' polluted air
every time you sit to bicker before me,
what I say to bend the torrent elsewhere
is drowned beneath waves of accusations
because sex with others when married
is the knife-wound that bleeds over both of you
until the break dryly takes. Your children
will suffer thru the rancor & wail
to be relieved,whether purgatorial or not
appealing to their well-being is fruit-less
unless the exploded yoke between you
can be balmed--could you hold hands
to let the tremor quiver all thru you
until it eases,let silence guide your eyes
one to the other to make plainer that love
festers & leaks beneath the squabbling & shame,
who is brave enough to jump into the deep end
to be bathed in this wasting pain? Our nation
could watch you do so & you would soothe
count-less others,it is the necessary sacrifice
for your muddled & sobbingly lost children,
do unto one another before claiming to save
their future,such voltage only over-loading you,
I am the better arrogance coaxing your transcendence.

                        April 25-27 & 29, 2005

BLAMING TASTES OF SHOWDOWN

What other man not always stronger
than you,my wife of these taming years,
our two young children the reigning proof
of your abiding devotion unto me
as who stays lovable after broken situs
      of even tragic happenstances,
I marryable & still changeable sooner
than decades later as commendably betrothed
          to a worshippable queen
           of impalpable grace aloft
from carriage upon my unaching back--
you the mother of our children & caretaker
of our home,no servile hireling but diligent
-ly cleaning & cooking while I work hard
each day,chatting thru dinnertime with you
as the sexual preface to what of us
steams nightly true. I love the muscular
-ly thrusting sports: football & hockey,
do not disturb me during these claiming games
on weekends when beer coats my innards
with shouting tongues of final victory,
women do not truly understand these manly acts
of bruising courage,since all of you whimper
when we press ourselves upon you to offer
what of us best commands you.
                            I live
in the feral tradition of hunters & warriors
hoisting our women to pull you thru the fires
of ancient manly wrath,puissantly proclaiming
our audacious worth to still be boldly heroic.

After an unsullyed courtship of passion
& amiable love,sooner than I never wanted
came the strafing insults & dour wounds
of jabbing & slapping me in once-a-whiles
before the kids but more so after they were older
than wailing babies fearing this raving man
borne out of this strange malice of marriage
thrust upon me as your wife of undeserving hurt,
beguiling our vows as steadfast Christians

that Commandments blossom as only holy
day after year. I am smaller yet wiser
than you, a woman outlasts a man's abject
-ly thrown temper to save what I fashioned
from nearly nothing,
      slowly annealed to you
over years to withstand such fury for myself
& our children until what irreparably snaps
sends me outward & ashamed. I lie again
to my friends & to doctors about your damage
upon me, my face swollen from the hard blows
after vomiting from your kicking my stomach
during dinnertime, when you coldly turn
  into some animal'd monster
as our children scream to be saved by God,
our Father who never told the Romans to bludgeon
Jesus for being Heavenly vatic.
        One night,
after you crack my jaw & freedom looms
louder as where we must feel our salvation,
the police order you to let me leave you
with what I own that is carryable in crisis—
so do not wait for my returning servitude,
since a woman unchains herself once a man
forges slavery thru his terms corrupting
her love as the indentured ruin of our promise,
the whole of love's history smashable between us.

      July 26-27, 2010

OUR IVY-CHOKED SIN CREEPING SKYWARD

How impalpably courageous we have lived,
thriving near the heart of marriage
's love & umbrage,for these long months
in bed when chance bends us closer
than wishes could render life as true
as you upon me, hugging & fucking
in some cocoon sheltering us from
your lovely wife & one of my better friends,
borrowing her husband for the pleasures
too long unrelieved in me since the traitor
that was my own husband slinked away
with his mistress to live long elsewhere
& some day marry her—-who outwits whom
in this creaking water-wheel of love
's smally-crazed knife-pricks I gift
to her despite my loving her kindness
to me for years,what she comes to know
of all of us beguiles our threesome's foolery.

You married her before I was sorely divorced
& I have watched your son & daughter
grow to be wonderful while playing together
where the middle-class spends lush weekends
in our neighbourhood—-far from any collapsing
Haitian earth-quakes rumbling the ground—-
I live several streets away & never dream
of taking the place of my good friend,
your wife—-it is not a second marriage
that I seek,rather a man who courts me
as a temptress to straddle the bounds
of rectitudinal matrimony,I a lissome
-ly big-breasted woman whose body welcomes
all you can offer the friend she cherishes.

We all live such calmer lives suburban
-ly pleasant & productive for ourselves
as doctor,nurse & realtor,as she
outgrew housewifery to begin selling homes
to professional patrons once your children

started school,I helping you with patients
every working day before we sneak time
as a man & woman merrily conjoined
to savour what spices more mundane meals
          as bodily apparitions
          in marriage's jumble
          of promise & bother
--once I fondled your cock at work,
you found a lover on either side
of you in the manly dream of woman
-ly worship,you well-saluting our devotion.

I strongly knew her before I befriended you,
we talked & shopped,she held me
after the traitor forsook me long ago
as sisterly as women whose hearts
keenly feel the aches of manly malice,
she said you were a finer husband
& was grateful to be so well-blessed--
so any envy swam shallowly in me
until you looked at me somehow entranced
in our daedal wishes to transgress
against her: sucking your cock deeper
than reason while you cupped my big tits
as how Plato was deflowered by Cupid
's stinger-pricks--I call her my friend
even now,since you love her for what I am not
& I love her for swallowing this brutal confusion.

        *

With no warning that either of you
would be home,I open the front door
to soon hear moaning of a womanly rapture
coming from our bedroom,unbeknownst to me
you are writhing in the throes of climax
from my husband,another fetid adulterer,
so I creep closer to see this commotion
to find both of you nakedly splayed
in the mid-afternoon heat in autumn
's first notice of summer's close,
the breeze thru the window unsweating you

& once all of our eyes lock,I feel myself
shaking as the smallest wifely tower
ruptured by the worst temblor of betrayal

's cloying clarity,
                    that he can fuck
my better friend in our bedroom caroling
        your coital hymn upraised
to Satan——which woman cries loudest
with a heaving bosom worthy of lament
& any pedigree of sin? How audacious
-ly charming was that lust-lost scene
of now ménage-a-trois in his dream
of Eastern bigamy,I double-crossed
by husband & friend purposely worthy
of deceiving me until I was worst-fooled
            finally there & then
            living your wily nightmare
for days & months since that awful afternoon,
having released my man to your avarice
        for ruining what hobbled you,
the best succour you could grant me being
*I sinned against you for the glory
of his sharable manly benevolence,regained.*

                    January 20-22,2010

OUR COCOON LESS BRUISED

for Karen

We salibriously knitted to riper goodness
while walking alongside Christian tenants
of charity,faith,worship & forgiveness
as two having come from rectitudinal families
where the dinner table was no battle-field
& manners are reflexsive unless necessarily
rejected in favour of freshly rest-less truth,
if *we were born into goodness & so raised*
then the world's daily mischief & distemper
startles us in this suddenly gaping crash-pit
between gifted mercy & tumbling skyscrapers
fire-blown to the ground because flagitious zealots
hard-maim American arrogance.
                                           Husband & wife
never dumbly corrupted by all that disrupts us,

we immured within our own notions of health
& mild righteousness to not waste ourselves
on plastic gluttony modernly offered as essential
-ly use-less garbage to the sententious primitives,
who hunted to eat to be belly-fed & never
disfigured more than with vulgar talk,we dying
randomly from machine guns & bomb-blasts
because the cowardice of hidden hatred cripples
the twitching victories of face to face. Nourishing food
more than sweets & chips to keep our blood clear
from clumped fat as we exercise to strain ourselves
harder than vegetal resting before television
's snoozing cackle,drinking little & no haze
from tobacco or hemp to cloud our minds
with organically pampering happiness
since our soul-holes must be filled with the world

's polluted beauty, there being no history
earlier than our lifetimes any longer that thrives
beyond beseeching museums. We go to bed
before midnight every night as sleep saves us

from wearier afternoons,no late-night talk shows
that are cartoons of conversation & selfish blather
is the name-sake of too many meetable people
in the day-time,Hollywood is an old junkie
whose fixes grow daily air-soaked & wretching.
Politics gathers its actors before the cameras
but the real work lingers where money is spent
& the news burrows beneath the skin of flinching
manly weather in ruptured prejudice & murder,
      the news of our world scars us every day

having awakened to rumours of rising paradise
tho we never foolishly risk ourselves as dare-devils
in scary rides or hurtling cars since injuries
can become the unfading signatures of idiots
trying to be stupidly famous,no contagious deficits
in our attention to death's devouring choke-hold
& so our dreams rarely black-bottom into nightmares
startling our hearts crazily awake. Going to church
eases the bland vacuum between our floundering
righteousness & images of Father & Son who lost
& regained life to blood-bathe our salvation,
so we give to those well-heartedly gifting to others
in famine or disasters to save mewling children––
yet comes the common confession unto each other
once it has burdened us again: our unfair judgment
of others hones our tongues with pricklish spite
against the poor,the ignorant & the blow-hards,
our good fortune lathers the pus of its abundance
& sends us shuffling from Golgotha with many
pocketed hands & whistling tunes of our reeking conceit.

                September 12-14, 2001

OUR MIDDLING AGE

for Karen

We say these birth-days are the tipping
toward death's welcoming us with nibbles
until our hearts boldly quit, age fifty
with thousands of days still owed us
before our life expectancy wanes into the aether,
if we are too young to die we are grayed
in the remembrance that time pokes our eyes
           to stop wasting pudgy time
to live bigger than regrets, we stronger
than those too lazy to abandon the couch
& eat better than such malignant fast food—
what of us has aged in looming grace
to be cherished or muscularly worked
to best our fear of moldering into putty
wheeled to the crowded ditch?
                     The mirror,
not bribed but truly kinder to us, says we are
the fairer ones of our softly middling age,
youth-full faces & few wrinkles to prove
well the startle of telling others how old
we claim to be, but our eyes require all sorts
of glasses to read print or study the full moon,
tho we hear well enough to bristle at the outpouring
noises of television or stores, which hate
silence's selling nothing. My memory wobbles
but walks in strides, it does limp forgetfully
as my mother in Heaven watches to place bets
on whether I will some day follow her higher
into the mind-less ozone. How the world
has a few of its aches hauled upon our backs,
relieved by lying prone & arching ourselves
to tense what lowly strains from the weight,
fearing the spasms from the unused muscles,
which cripple us for days as we curse God
for cruelly tricking us. My shoulder ached
with the frozen menace of a swelling corpse
unable to shave or praise, x-ray'd & injected
to restore its tenure, all of me huddled to balm
what so use-lessly drooped. Our hands grip

tightly to carry & unscrew,firm hand-shakes
for all deserving so,my hand-writing scribbles
its gibberish to be poorly translated by anyone,
our skin dry in the wintertime,tho our hands fondle
what of each other uprises. Our hearts pump
firmer than basking laziness,we run or swim
to push our lungs to hoarse yelps of succour,
our stomachs not bulging to tumorous midriff
& laughable flab-rolls,never swallowing a beach-ball
& forgetting to vomit its waste. What tames
my desire for you in the wintertime as I olden
to feel strangely chaste,testosterone dissolves
until the sun warms my crotch enough
to pester you,finding your own climax
with frantic fingers to be cruelly elusive-—
it is our joy to prod passion between us
& this down-swell says our gaining age
must be forestalled longer than merely possible,
surely not yet this end for us. Sprained ankles
& toenail fungus,tho I keep walking briskly
all the time,always wanting to be able
to chase the robber or rapist who corrupts us,
so our wooden trail is raked to lure us
to well-shape ourselves thru our later years,
going on older than paling wishes.
                                        Youngly old
we rise each morning & groan our stiffening age,
how to get limber before work,how to live
puissantly able to bolster our health in ways
            necessary to benignly thrive,
how to remain the plainest living miracles
as we olden into the wrinklish majesty
of who we must be-—other than on birth-days
we must curdle our fears into promises
to live with the fullness of baby'd immortals.

                    January 9-11, 2006

OUR SILVER ANNIVERSARY,HEART-FULLY UNTARNISHED

for Karen

How you came before me,innocently facing
what in me longed for a big-breasted,
pretty young woman to have & to hold
over the days of my lifetime cherishably fine,
walking together the shortest distance
to where I could begin to grasp what
in you relieved the stringy loneliness
in me,having watched other couples kiss
on the beach in the long wintertime,
when the sun bores into our sad eyes
& pierces our love-lack hard. So much
driving over the next couple of years
to date on the weekends to raise myself
into you or slouch thru our boredom
in a small town restless in our twenties
to learn of the world,you taught me
how to save money & I nuzzled you
with studenty humour,when does the alchemy
between men & women roast & percolate
to bond us monogamously--I too cheap
to buy you an engagement ring,abruptly
proposing marriage while planning a trip,
it was a social simpleton you married
amidst flowers on a bright autumn morning
25 years ago,tho I spouted wisdom later
once I could boil myself forward as a man.

Where we lived lengthened over the years
thru three houses in two neighbouring states
to allow for badminton on summer evenings
behind the cramped apartment marriage
first bestowed us in a smaller town drawling
its slower pace to find us at the laundromat,
if rarely ever again. Eventually we found
the woods to live comfortably with fireplaces
& room to play,first shaded on all sides
but with sky-lights to see blue & black
aspects of weather,always the piles of leaves

to rake as the gnashing slaves to autumn
's brown-spilt wilting from count-lesss trees
hauled to the dump or thrown deeper into
the woods to magically disappear by springtime,
a woodstove lifting warmth thru the floor
to our bedded busyness. Then the largest
& most elegant house in a shady subdivision
where we were pestered by barking dogs
owned by neighbours friendly unto themselves,
toting firewood over the carpet surrendered us
to gas logs later, I painted the outside
by the cul-de-sac thru a sweaty August
after being laid-off by friends of youths
incorrigibly writhing aloud.
                                        A log palace
our huntable dream for suitable land
finally found in a locale we had never
tramped thru until the newspaper ad
said it was perfect, & it surely was:
five-plus wooded acres, upon which we built
a growing baby over five months in soggy wintertime
in a Republican back-water whose history
said time could crawl forward slowly enough
to feel its innocence pleasurably real,
we shielded by greenery from the piercing sun
until the leaves fall again to work us further
into the realm of Her barest-named trancery.

How swiftly aroused our ardorous kinship
as such loving chemistry hatched in the laboratory
of our hearted testimony of your face
unto my yang-spun adoration of you
kissably sure   what webbed concordance
forming once our spines align to proceed
about cars, houses & the baby who would fail us
after years of deciding later than biology
recommends for any of us   other women
tease me with breasted prettiness walking
away from this compass-root of fidelity
's clutching me firmer than merely looking
momentarily elsewhere, you see me watching them
but I walk in your stride before caressing
your blessed specialness   my fourth name
is humouring you once your life sudden

-ly stiffens into the womanly grumpiness
your gender proclaims as your sufferage,
since men have barely understand pregnancy
& witnessing child-birth still for those chosen
few who can stomach miracles tell me
my cock relieves your cunt's itch & your tits
fill my hands with the joy of lippy fucking,
there being no gossip worthy of woman
-ly wonder that any male homosexual
can not even conjure as the truest way
to satisfy our lives first your father
& then my mother went to the fortress
of Heaven's increate mercy to be relieved
of what we lose past more than ailing
daily & nightly,letting us know our patience
for such will gell in the bad circumstances
Death fingers & shapes upon us
                                          how ineffable
your tender countenance once I prick you
to me as singularly as marriage demands
in the genial foreplay of my man to your woman
as kissing eclipses into our catty twilight.

October 8-10, 2007

WHOSE LOVE LIFELY CONSCRIPTED

for Karen

How early in childhood were you stretched,
tautly yet hardly mewling,between
mother & father thru summers & winters
from implacable demands to stay smiling
-ly perfect,how squashed between
one grown-up heart & one grown-up mind
melding thru such words of prickly encouragement
to learn & behave better than all others
until your life would well-resemble theirs:
gnashing on scraps of happiness & wonder
-ing what is clutchably fair. Alcoholism,
stoicism,guilt-trips & an abhorrence
for fun kept you open-mouthed but rarely
shame-fully silly——I may not have survived
how you lived in this private hell-vice
of sisterly silences & parental dictums
presenting love as a teachable abstraction
while sullying what a child's heart knows
to be true: *to be hugged & confirmed*
says love is the gift from anyone
who pours yourself upon me cherish
-ably well,so daily lend me what of you
knits my soul's start.
                        The girl-friends
& ignorance about boys,photos of shy smiles
& the teary rancor of being unfairly scolded
after cleaning or your averager grades,
no Olympic athlete or TV singing star
but rather the smartest of these sisters
who now dodges your melancholy mother
on the telephone how many decades later,
my male advice not flexible in your limbs
to render her human by stuttering your heart
as the princess who mangles the Queen's crown.

How stretched between their old withholding
& shackling your life-love to be a grown-up
during & after college before I met you,

sadder & plainer from their tonnage upon you
crawling so slowly thruout your bigger body
to shelter you from drunken dorm-life
& asking few questions akin to *How are you
doing as our young woman still so innocent
-ly living,* one daughter smarter
than obvious soul-rot stumbling over the campus,
always a virgin amidst secret co-ed orgies
widening the communal gap between students
& fretting parents whose babies strolled aloud
as composted offspring.
                          How much did you
feel mother & father wander about your body,
did you want to shed the skin of their countenances
thru any worsening umbrage telling them
     *you raised but not saved me
     from your bodily commentaries*
while driving to the small town to begin
your first job, unable to wash them
off your skin because they burrowed
far deeper than any mere cleansing
could rinse away—-before I met you
this inching parental infection hosted itself
in your body amidst laughter & fickle love,
but you offered how much of yourself
freely to risk their advice or scorn,
stretched upon your bed with a strange man
who fondled his students, & then wanting
to ask Daddy if he is worthy to date
at all, girlishly asking: *Who will tell me
about the world, now that I left home
& am easy prey to be shocked again?*

          *

Can a mother stretch a grown daughter
from both ends of you once your father
dies yet survives thru your dimmer empathy
unto me as the husband who gifts you
my sacrificial manliness beyond his letter
telling you to raise yourself? The cross
between suffering her on the telephone
& brow-beating my mischief as a wife

-ly nun stings me as a daughter
's cowardice to shrink her royalty
in the pellucid pry-work of your gain-say
over their sodden weight upon you—-
whose Queendom eclipses the other's
in this hopscotch with no finish line,
so must I topple both of you by leaving
the woman I love?
                      No plainer apologies
but plenty of menopause,you still being
the smartest sister whose reflexsive rebuttals
too-rarely rouse me now,mother or father
never sorrow-full to you for their style
of lady-raising & so I do quickly flinch
in this contagion of the lightly damned,
your fourth name having become *arrogance*
as spelled in swelling capitals atop my heart
's separation papers,
                          divorce the stupidity
of my losing you over their malnourishment
of you: surely no whitest African refugee
but hungry nevertheless,so what are
your womanly gifts unto me,older than fifty?

                              August 25-27, 2009

BEFORE YOU LEAVE

for Karen

I having praised you for well-outlasting
what your mother & father served you
as a youngster as more than three meals
    of prickly comments & unconfirming
-ly cherishable love,having seen myself
their selfish & stoic manner before & after
death's rendering us smaller than gossip
could blossom again,I could not live
with their tourniquet cramping your soul
& their stiffer blessings tarnish you still
despite our many years of alembical marriage,
since the unconscious savours the poison
of all thrust upon us. Added to this damage
has been the years of hormonal up-thrust
-ed menstrual & now menopausal coarseness,
dour enough to thrash beneath my skin
on days when estrogen unmercifully deserts you
to meld history into a past,present & future
    called *you who worsens my life*
until what cleaves in me is love from survival,
tho it is still in minutes & not over days
or months,for that I am bravely grateful
but my love for you drunkenly stumbles
its favour thru the mottled testimony
sweating on your face how many times
every day,husbands taken for granted
by wives entitled to grumpily fault us
for nearly nothing, & you no wiser afterward.

Our blood-bulging umbrage,one to the other
once your hormones surge the length of you
& how the world must daily say your name,
your love of banked money & how my jokes
mainly escape you,yours a denser mind
parentally immuring,too much prickliness
& yet how lovable otherwise—-I love you
but what chafes me is your fickle favour
of me,hormones or not,entitled to jab me

with slim gifts of yourself upon me
in wifely fondness, all enraptured too rarely
for nearly thirty years, hormones or not,
hating music & blaming church for bothering you
as tho either should worship you as the Queen
of Bored Royalty, how creative are complaints
without Art, happiness in the next day's mail
newly addressed to you—-tho it is you who says
you want to leave me & live alone "for a while,"
solipsism for all three meals & the dessert
of me on the weekends?   What will roil you
forward is to shrink the gap between us by tasting
your dis-ease with people thru healing touches
as offered by Jesus to sinners who strayed
from God's Word: simplest, to pet our cats
until they play-fully en-trance you to love
their slippery devotion to us, to let them
walk thru your legs & to sniff your face,
to be invaded by their feline curiosity & demands
to be petted until they satedly ignore you,
               thus love in their quirky favour
which behooves you as the giver of their smiledness,
their tails thanking you.   Then know I am
a huge cat to fondle with your words & deeds,
give until I must also give & our circuit
grows charged—-no more stanger-looks in bed—-
I need a woman whose currency never bankrupts
& whose recessions rebound upon my cloyed lap,
telling me I am the last man who so emboldens you.

June 8 & 10, 2009

II

Not Yet, Go Back

AT THE BOTTOM OF MY WELL

I stand after sitting till the cramp-jerks upright me to pace barely one step in this circular purgatory eight feet below the ground's unresonant celibacy to leave the world for one warm afternoon to feel immured in concretic blandness to hum or shout any malaise into the sky-bright aether,not punished but my wife will lend me the savoured rope to escape later than modern preferences can yet swallow,you my breasted saviour from this echoing mesmer-palace.

Bless again such blue-hued respite from the coldest weather the last month of a winter whipping down from Canada's wrath that hockey too rarely oozes in prime time, this shelter favourable against savage tornadoes or sqall-flung hurricanes wrecking our fortune by thrusting thru our houses,home-less weather revaged upon us after midnight once sleeping trembles in the summertime because dying writhes thru our back-tossed minds. You told our children Daddy is part of a science project studying the effects of a collapsed world upon our psyches,I awakening to a shrunken territory no larger than where we can turn & fear—it is really to miss all three of you enough to forget later where I now am,married into fatherhood at the cost of this fakely singular transcendence,rather committed to raise our son & daughter with an earnest respect for what rashly matters in the wrinkled envelope holding all of our snipped instructions. We teach them that love conquers nothing but soothes the mis-steps & even the falls,that my love for you lets them stand atop its sturdier know-so to walk & run elsewhere beyond its certainter knowledge,its lingering sense in their hearts oldening them into the here-after. Those who beat or molest their own children must give their soul-less contagion to those whose little lives they too well remember,it was buried in their hearts & flushed to the back-side of their lives to hibernate until their offspring could suffer such,who would not want to thrash a mother or father for bruising or fucking a son or daughter before bedtime,a pubescent girl orgasmic from her own father's erectest mischief? This the whimpering personal politics of mere survival,children enslaved to work wherever brutish men demand their tamer labour,women clothed in anonymous bodies untouched in public so no man will be erectly tempted, who still can not read at all in this clamantly chattering hyper-world & so hides their mind in a ditch recovered only in dreams? No other American would court the penury of this dry-well'd hollering spot, I do not brag for myself but recall those who have never drowned in any real besting success, all the forgotten & wasted ones. Americans are luckier than even our unashamed imaginations: the plentiful produce at the supermarket & all the cash in our bank accounts before its spillage at the shopping mall or the car dealership—politics hovers above our bodies ready to infect us with viruses of mouthable righteousness, but politics dies before the crucified corpse of Jesus, His empty tomb our untasted promise of redemption from sins only half-red & sweating. Fifty years past crying thru my labour & two years past her senile death from an invalid's small-boned inertia, my mother rests in Heaven & watches me carry her face thru the world, dementia the end-less mental rock-slides of forgetful lapses overtaking her brain & those of so many old people whose blank stares are full of no compassing stars, spare me this vacant oblivion the size of a personal galaxy to still speak to you as we sit on the porch of the nursing home, humming rock-&-roll as statuing air guitars as frozen baby-boomers whose sunset is always looming. A room full of old people renders me tremblish, their bingo & story-telling so slowly done the world might die & be re-born, how could I come to live in such a facility unless I too had succumbed to their pace of frailty's snaring them alive, such is happening to others, tho I forget their names. Older or still younger, who willingly makes the necessary art thru this time of warfare & global warming, I write & listen & read & watch all of it, these soul-sent messages of alembical scripture up-raising ourselves out of composted monotony, art will outlast even television for a lucky few, its boxed comedy fashioning the fewest masterworks, tho the elderly love its noisy convenience. It is the young mothers & fathers, the too-busy workers whose creativity was sapped before any remembrance, no coaxing & no classes, no instruments committed to making despite busyness & lamer inspiration, how to yank newness out of ourselves with the slippery ease of our ripest being, how we even breathe our uniqueness. He came to touch our hearts with the hands of God, it is the only oldest story camped & re-told at the back of our minds for all these centuries, Jesus the nagging Messiah pecking upon

us with His bloody miracles & stories, He no body-sized art-work but the wandering canvas beseeching us to gift ourselves to others as the life swallowing art & offering seeds to souls. Our faith fades in the abstract absence of His glory on earth,we were never His disciples & that difference tempts us from every-elsewhere,going to church being the wobbly mid-way between doubt & faith,but faith must have its stones to feel & not just the stories of the most courageous man-god to be sacrificed for us,can we thank Him only with our faith? My resurrection would be to climb out of this chosen hole as a man relieved of the worst of myself to lend to others some of my grown soul to be healed of slivers of malaise & fear,this is when I feel Him reach thru me to roil their scourge to shed it lightly,since such places of resurrection are named with sudden fortune.
   As the afternoon cools & you return to rescue me from my limpest torture,I look up at you to silently say:

monks are cowards to always live
this way,sheltered from the world
's blasting tragedies,but let us borrow
their safe-places enough to gather
ourselves to return to what startles us
every day again,
    let me walk thru you
as the least sententious sooth-sayer
born after television to somehow up-raise us
  into His Son's tragic-glory,
church being the first place on the walk
to the mirage that teases our faith-fullness,
will it harden into Heaven when we die
as that tunnel of light the stories tell
welcoming us before saying: *Not yet,go back.*

      February 19-22, 2007

MYTH WRITHING INTO LIFE

This loving pool of water-rhyming shine
beholds him the wet caress of wonder
looking down from the soul-less eyes
of Narcissus, loved better than another
only reflectively so, no sex wanted
but rather the love mirrored from
whose pure-gracing heart to a young man
's longing face, not mother or father
who could inexhaustibly give forever
a love untarnished by temperament
or desire—not girls coaxing his lust
but rather an angel's white-lit love
chosen by God for his ever-lasting heart,
grander than coincidence or alibis
or false promises, sex-lessly dying
because such water-rhyming swoons him
into its spell of cracked-hollow perfect love—
all I need spelled with outstretched arms
met not by love but by mirror-water,
so he dies needing the blessings of perfection
unclutched at dusk once his magic also dies.

Not merely ancient myth writhing in me,
since I do not sit gazing at brackish water
for hours while conjuring the impossible:
no love purely reflective & self-lessly hovering,
what swells missing truly gnaws at my heart,
& tho I will not die from any such
hearted starvation, surely a leaf-less tree
feels its shivering wintertime.
        My lack
comes from the curse of being special
as the only child of parents & grandparents
long enough to be babied with sturdy cuteness,
it comes from the tongue-lashes of righteous
-ly surly parents who said I was older
than the calendar & that I was wiser
than purest childhood, so I lived with how
they sugared or salted me tho it was
always only me, even my stuffed play-room

loomed larger than any truer kinship
with kids my age,so his water-rhyming
rings in my heart but not so hug-melded
& confirming,since the mirror lies
once I walk away to be stroked or shaken
by our kind-lying world. A "bubble-head"
I have been called by my friends & my wives,
insultingly true as I tap its glassy thickness,
what is the humour outside my own laughter
as God birthed me earlier than the Flood.

Who looks to stare into another's soul,
my eyes going where my own heart sends me
& not into the murky business of others,
I tell you all that I deem necessary
for your simplest enlightenment since I teach
students to think beyond the tight measure
of school-books,I grew into our world fuller
than penury's blind-folds,can you follow
all I bountifully offer? Both of my wives
said I lost them with my abstracter ramblings
about politics,fairness & womanly impotence
suffered from men—my son lives elsewhere
& hugs me at holidays,I often get told
he favours me despite years of geography
tho being worshipped by any of them
embarrasses me,whomever she was too phony
& I scolded her so,women seem to tire
of my hollow chatter but it is medicinal
to be bravely truth-told—now it is this
loveliest woman who has at last befriended me
& understands my beguiling style,it is you
prodding me to write this very public letter
asking for forgiveness & greatest patience,
since any bubble-head must be slowly cracked
to feel fresh sun-light all across my tender scalp.

How you behold me better than anyone else
yet have me struggle to give to you
            more than my customary nothing,
I heart-flexed & panting while doing so
in looking & listening with no receipt
of myself sooner than I can breathe

in relief of such torture,immured in myself
feeling his heart-rhyming pool shrivel
in me quicker than any steadier standing
until you clutch me in gifted thanks
for o'er-leaping myself. Any woman
who mothers me so must be well-loved
rendering me sweatingly special unto myself
in bursting out of the bubbled confines
of me for these awful minutes of
     courting you as my salvation-
who else alembically charged thru this thunder
-ously hearted maelstrom of wriggling
myself into giving unto someone so special
that you hover as my angelic halo,
I grander than disaster still.
                         All of this
for me in my forties,younger than wisdom
's fossiled knowledge only readable before,
I cherish your beauty now made famous
thru my heart's gossip as my bubble
daily shrinks to love another glowingly so.

                August 6-9, 2007

CREAKY & LEAKING

Who else's summers not otherwise loving
before where we gathered so far out West
with painted faces & flowers in our hair
to listen to how our music had blossomed
thru the songs of so many bands suddenly
roiling the putty of our young lives
            into cascading day-stories
abrading us from the weight of our parents
to love ourselves thru nights of moments
first at Monterrey & later on at Woodstock,
loving what happens in the self-same magic
youth nourishes as how the ideal alembic
-ally triumphs before dying slower than
we finally remember. We loved ourselves
mostly with drugs, since without drugs
we could not inhale our coarser selfishness,
as one stabbed another to death in a crowd
in front of a band who demanded shelter
from our sober atrocities. You said we never
obeyed or worked hard enough, were too lazy
& Heaven-bent, we laughed & cursed at you
for never understanding how we soul-fully
differed from you, being mantic magicians
casting spells to haul joy back from the graves
        of your straight-laced regrets
-if not truly the clever children of God,
we spent our time chasing ragged images
of how He looked & lived, our louder world
cracking the monasteries hiding the chosen
to drag you into our unrepentant pleasures.

How long our hair grew even while
living at home to irk your rectitudinal
-ly prized lackeydom as the standard
            against which our perfidy
                thrashed & eventually abandoned
your hosting our wayward lives too tightly,
our blurry clothes & staying out on farms
to grow crops Naturally resonant in our bellys,

having traveled thru minded correspondence
to where you never ventured.
                                      What the press called
the generation gap, how wide these river
-y tantrums between fathers & your offspring
borne of how time wavers our sentiments
toward such riving calamities of sense & purpose,
we visited enough to not be fondly forgotten
but softly died between times. Neither of us
proudly sanguine about bombing the Vietnamese,
as children wailed from napalm over the roads
as half their country ate the wisdom of the other—-
younger than certain we read *New Left Notes*
as the wiser propaganda authored by someone
besides LBJ or Nixon, we hotly battling
in Chicago because the draft nearly killed us
in a war sullying America's honour to spare
the holy value of freedom upon those innocents.

After the war help-lessly strangled to death,
many of us married & raised our children
over three decades before turning fifty years old,
twenty years into the vacuous territory
of being untrustworthy & choked with history,
we had school & careers, spouses & divorces
& told our children they could live as they wished
as tho life was a happy democracy crowned
upon every kid's head, telling them they were
wonder-full even after they disobeyed & failed us,
discipline the evaporating sand-line memorable
for what only rarely happened. We loved cocaine
& knew those with too many sexual diseases,
shouldering Republican dogma in straying
from our ideals to taste the bile of prejudice
'd rhetoric once Nixon was finally impeached
& Carter set himself on fire in the desert,
millions of canaries cackling over the years
that Jesus was a Democratic fool. Our children
found a third parent in junky'd video games
& left home only to return after college
as the teen-agers who grew sideways,
scolding their drug usage as worse than ours
in the aching epicycle of self-destruction

gifted thru Mexico & Afghanistan,we became
the mistakes our parents never lamely made
thru the wealth of our arrogant mirror-cracks.

The eldest of us sixty years old,now long ago
in our restless time since all the festivals
ended & joy became fashioned once by one
at a time again,we having grown fatter
thru the gluttony from all the marketing poured
upon us since babyhood as the sellable generation
corporations have loved to own. We grew tired
after all the exercising so hard for years
once our bodies reminded us youth sorrow
-fully wanes with the grace-less excesses
Heaven never promised us. We grew rich
& bought everything love demanded of us
in the warped charity of selfish benevolence
gnashing in the bellys of the aged & the poor,
parking our SUVs in front of the nursing homes
but visiting ourselves so seldom. We got Obama
after the Bushes,Clinton also got impeached
for free love & the world daily mocked us
as tho menopause & retirement are sellable
for the price of breakfast,our moldering
captured on cable television in reality shows
edible as the bad snacks for votive dieters,
the clergy stopped tapping our frozen shoulders
years ago to feel God in the poverty of our purchases,
kneeling unto no one.   The few vatic ones
pulled our dreams & the paths to reach them
back inside your lives to finger the cultural winds
                    & bravely let them die,
trusting only those whose wisdom is fatter
than our bellys,traveling back to the fields
where history surrenders to the emptiness
of what may yet be born,accidentally magical.

August 24-27, 2010

MUSCULAR KNOTS OF POVERTY

Well later than Christmas' merry-romp
of ringing cheer & pennies in kettles,
you invite me into your shamblish trailer
(more mobile than only traveling disaster)
too close to where I live in our county
of rural prejudice & certain generosity
to witness how the poor daily survive
not only during this menacing recession
but years ago when the rich wasted cash
        in gangrened gluttony,
your family cramped in this single-wided,
sun-claimed misery where hope itches
to name itself at all worthy. Young parents
with youngest children: a toddler & a baby,
no high school diploma feelable between you
& so man works with your learning hands
to feed your housewife & unplanned children,
the jobs never oddly unworkable since money
flavours the bread & milk in your bellys,
the old factory work long ago shipped overseas
        where the poor are crazily grateful
for coins per hour, while your welfare checks
& Medicaid say Western opulence dimly shines
in how you are qualified to be wobbly counted
as charitably gifted of what our own poor
deserve as how we bear Jesus' burden upon us.

Poverty tasted blood-lessly cruel before
breakfast after sleep's raging demands
for fairer wealth until dinnertime's fretting
over money & repairs, your stern eyebrows
heavy with the worry of crumpled magic
in stretching food & coins farther than
bestly necessary, I hear your tempers
simmering & curdling in the summertime heat
from what all the television shows promise:
wealth is what prayers suddenly deliver
into the hands of those mercifully blessed

*by God's reigning favour,He up-raises you
toward His claiming Kingdom.*
                              What you fix
serves to save you further money-aches
but going to the doctor stumbles your parentage
of these two youngest ones,they too sick
too often to stay in this hot-house shack
in catching the fever of earliest malaria,
who all sweats after night-fall trembles
from sickness & bills,so never fear to go
to any healer who stares at you plainly
with suspicious glimpses & ornery lectures,
since your ignorance of everyday health
can not be tamed only within this pestilence
named as your chaining squalour. Any politics
is borrowed from relatives or television
to simplify worldly discord into facts & lies
tellable to anyone who proudly thinks so little,
            thus other contagious Republicans.

The moldy stench of the trailer coughs
tubercular heaving in all four torsos
once summer surrenders to icy winter
on nights when dreams of tropical islands
burn & melt thru such coarse hypnosis
curing no pain nor balming realer hope,
bread & milk hurlable out the back door
except for your bellys' language shouting
its gasping rancor: *we were never fools
for living so lowly,no gambling idiocy
twitching from lost wealth elsewhere,
& prayers heard by God from our lips
crumble before midnight.*
                          How moral
-ly righteous is a blind man maddened
for eye-sight that he would not pluck them
from a dead man,so you tell her again
about your scheme to rob the local store
with a gun borrowed from a relative
sitting in prison,the bank too risky
with its cameras but she reminds you
that without your petty cash they starve

thru shivering nights while you'd eat well
in lock-up in another county unaffordable
in day-light—-staring at the gun
lacking bullits & ample manly courage,
you lay down amidst them in the living room
to dream of abandoned riches on islands
unclaimed by criminals more culpable
than you: a wiser man, rocking & weeping.

March 3-5, 2009

ACCORDIAN STEPS

What comes from one green leaf could
hardly ruin my life with spiked rushes
of freshest air when snorted as powder
-y white kindness bound to lend travel
        to the least righteous woman
younger than any wisdom's flourishing favour,
having spent end-less days over several years
flaring my nostrils to be grandly transported
to white-shining nirvana faster than love
's testy fidget-struts,since at all times
it stokes the vacuum of this modern sufferage
with bright fire & will never kill me—-
I am not stupid with it: I still work
every day,tho my face some weekday mornings
melts the mirror with my picturesque wreckage
moldering to well-scold me. Being still single
in my 30s,there is no baby bulging my heart
to whimper verses of motherhood's diaper-songs,
but my parents tell me to visit only when sober
& Christmas lends me its crucifixional birth
of repentance's half-stammer,momently puissant
to heed your advice that real life is never
soaked in cocaine, I your worst-won child
thus place a wager that by next Easter
Jesus will die & be re-born not only
in Heaven but also amidst my aging weeds
to haul me out of my paradise back to where
pleasure swarms from gnawing on trees while waiting
for a husband to slip beneath my skin to wifen me.

After another last damage on New Year's Eve,
I sit in this circle of anonymous children
older than our excuses & wiser than death,
whose hearts burst in some midnight emergency room
because the amount of powder blurred in the dark,
so we chat & give our soliloquies to mild applause
as the palest mothers & fathers for we incorrigibles
annealing ourselves in dawn-steps. I can stay
straight for days,work & my friends fitting
a head-band as a daily compass to feel the sun

on my soul-lessness,   sometimes I stare
at lines of talcum powder after a shower
& can not accept my favourite foreign country
is jettable only from coca leaves,no vacation cheaper
than lisping addiction,servile to its peculiar rules
of flights & queasy down-time--soon seven nights
cleaner than white-fire ecstacy,no chips yet
tho I am circled by all manners of collapse,
disasters smeared on their faces as you watch
behind them as my sighing guardians.
                                        30 days
pass as my birth-day looms & I tongue the chip
as the plastic wafer for a soiled Catholic
who left the Church & found transcendence
in a Ziploc bag,coke fits anywhere
its powdery & shape-less profundity
roils my lapsed happiness with its warp-aid
unto *The Saving Place:* between earth & Heaven
thrives the sky's basking majesty--some nights
I ache for its fervor after being stranded
for weeks with these duller weed-wacks plaguing me
to feel the breadth of all my heart is offered,
         life how coyly tyrannical

while listening to their pukey stories of wailing
spinal spillage as the flaming contagion of ingrates
coarsely cheated of love's soothing hands & kisses,
pity bubbling up in this circle of stand-ins
auditioning for the role of Alembically Best
& dying of life-fright. I am told to be relieved
of my powdery friends & any other drunkards
sapping my abstinence to greet deep loneliness
with high-fives,how many trite phrases
          illumine "the hole in my soul"

as fillable with the trash of our unblessed envy,
one day at a time born seventy years ago
between two men who could not wait for Freud
to cure them--how to reach Ash Wednesday
without so much roughage,on my birth-day
I snapped & snorted just enough to remember,
so no chip at 60 days as I know this vortex

roars several times each week: *I need cocaine
worse than love,* call me its worst servant.

Into the Lenten season with fewer slips
than deserved,I go to Mass after work
where the usual cadre of old people pray
& meekly sing to recall Jesus' suffering
on the Cross,my light from Heaven thus far
pellucidly gifted as rebounding from relapse
          in my wettest curiosity flailing
after weeks of growing sick of myself sober--
if real life becomes boring after too long a while,
what to do? My parents can not love me
out of drugs,they can not fill the hole
any longer with measured advice & hugs,
what of my future hardens into that drenching me
with joy-full soul-rain, fresh-born
as a ground zombie of our risen Lord,
where found His miracles in anyone's soul
swearable unto me?   Bitter white powder
Naturally ecstatic,lifted for Jesus to snort
on the Cross to see God before Heaven
's grandeur greets You,had I done so
would You have rebuked my ignorance
about cocaine as a false idol before God--
on the first nights,I lay spread-eagled
on the bed to fidget this poison out of me,
hardly sleeping,I thought of You hanging
from the torturous tension between earth & sky
& cried of my forsaking coke for malaise
unmercifully so,since I will not die from
       the worst junkie's recklessness
       full of such nadiring wastage-

on Black Friday,I grow cleaner than chaining betrayal.

                        October 19-21 & 24, 2005

AFTER THE WAR

blooms the nightly death of my better sleep
from sneezes & sirens even after months
of civilian rest from such pressing weaponry
fired from the lapsed consciences of zealots
thwarting our democracy to kill each other
          with Muhammed's permission
to vanquish the freedom of commonly-gaped
mouths yearning only to speak specks of bounty
borrowed from the stockpiles of their conjurings—
what I remember of Iraq sweats & shivers
after dark beneath a trained fortress roiling
to break into air as the news most eluding me.

I started working again at the plant making
what machinery can not kill their civilians
with its heavy potential,not haulable upon
their backs to be smuggled deep into the desert
& shoulder-fired behind their masks of disaster
along the roads we suffered to save a nation,
my co-workers' questions about the war answered
not with white-wash but until they blanch
& I return to work,I younger than their years
on the job as veterans of the union struggles,
having fought longer than I to survive
beyond the orphans in the alleys in Baghdad
begging for milk & cigarettes,hanging onto our legs
until as fathers we had to scatter them elsewhere.

From the watery distance of calamities
sanctioned by ornery men I daily dreamed
of your loveliness & our beautiful young son
          as my graspably lovable *home,*
peering at both of you thru the computer screen
was the night-time ache of soldiers longing
to caress who best claims our purpose,
yet now I hear the stories of my brethren choking
their women during delirious sleep & a few killing
their wives so soon after returning from the ruin:
as tho what looms terrorably close could be found

42

upon the body of a woman strokable when alone,
she the venomous enemy,the children killed,
the dusty crawling of death-time. You do say
I have changed,that the war as my clutched secrets
is the life chewing itself within a man's soul
witnessed but abandoned once my orders came
to leave to re-marry you & to raise our son,
five years old who mouths lessons from kindergarten
& jumps into my lap as the demi-orphan knowing
his fatherly surprise has at last come home. The war
has become my menstruation,pregnancy & menopause,
what women never suffered until you wanted
your share of the hemorrhaging flesh-bust of war,
the fourth world found world-wide in this
devilish century the worst weaponry has fashioned
to kill those who never asked to bravely change us.

           *

What testier reckoning warfare demands
from young soldiers sheltered with ropish hope
unraveling from the first day's pacificer
spat out to safely hustle out of the way
of all incoming fire-harm. It was every day
on patrol the mortar-fire or bomb-blasts
christened us so close or thru the stories
of our brethren lost anywhere in this desert-dump
-brushing my teeth killed another soldier
in the distance—-survivor-guilt collared us
& fell to the ground at dawn,we had to go
to where demon-men slaughtered their own populace.
Our hearts froze & thawed on & off patrol
thru the gangrene of this corpsed scenery,
witnessing the slow-steady end of the world
until we left for the heaven that is America,
saluting no greater purpose than to merely live
as those moldered by war's hissing infection
rampantly savaging our minds with the song:
No sameness left,surely no saneness left,
war is the traitor soul-claimed. How impalpable
any of this to civilian eyes & ears,we can not
expect you to deeply know what bleeds your senses,
who else but soldiers could become fully annealed

to death-rips lasting for hours in the heat,
that those for whom we fight would kill us

because democracy spelled backwards is victory.

Machine gun-fire & RPGs whiz & burst
above our heads while hunkered in a shack
blasted from its schooling where insurgents
curse our alembical presence calling them outward
to face our palest hatred closer than dogma,
neither the first nor the last of these fights
to rule what of the desert redly proclaims us
            the master of smaller tragedies--
no time for dreams of home-show or the birth
of friends' babies,what pops out is the sudden
-ly lasting damage of our soldiers shot in the neck
or shrapnel'd to death,what twirls in this circus
are the minutes & hours of our hearts stuttering
to even breathe,spitting gun-fire & always ducking,
if not such gnashing manly help-lessness this shit
spells the names of fresh nurse-maids.
                                        I bolt up
in the bed sweating the after-math of vengeance
masked in white garb & blood-silly slogans,
this whirl-wind tossed into our purpose
while defending against the collapse of a country
governed by generals & zealots,my friends
maimed or killed *is* the war of my length here,
where the wrestling match nightly happens
is this un-numbed tonnage of our lives trembling
but savagely sure: to save us & to kill them,
the sworn enemy of our tolerance,what I dream
after pulling my comrades out of their fire
is to pick them off coming at us & pile their corpses
into the testimony of war's best failure,
         that killing solves all the problems
         other men grease with their ideas--
so I choke who does not die from my gun-fire
until time rolls into the cornered innocence
of every soldier leaving States-side to disappear
into his dreams of back-firing civilization--

*after the war,we soldiers implode our redemption
into bursts of clenched transcendence,distanced
farther than the crib,my favourite work-shop,
since we heard no good songs the entire time.*

                    March 8-9,13 & 15, 2006

OUR 4,000 SOLDIERS PATROLING HEAVEN

You volunteered after the towers collapsed
as the blasting crow-bar to pry out patriotic
-ally flavoured service unto our country
in being sent to where the terrorists hissed
as mobile fangs from Saddam Hussein
's torturing mouth & from the Taliban
's Satanic worship to kill all Americans,
magnetic resonance in the hearts of soldiers
who grew annealed to how such zealots
bent their weaponry thru words & deeds
to spread dis-ease while slyly grinning
over the spoils of their curses. Their venom
full of sleeping sickness,nausea once in bed
from fear-sung blood-rage,you half-glad
to go to Khandahar,Fallujah or Baghdad
over five years of soul-sucking combat
to kill their hatred for us thru this war
's caustic hemorrhages of bomb-screams
upon the civilians & as well-thought upon you
in this miasmic savagery of god-less carnage
from the grandsons of Saddam's old mayhem,
tho how do you kill the host of the hydra
's legs that daily reincarnate?
                        Generals
& lesser soldiers have moved you all around
the country in this most drunken game of chess,
they having learned Vietnam is not repeatable
unless the hatred of any long-squatting army
on their soil can not be daedally extrapolated
from Hanoi to Anbar Province over 30 years
as the telepathic message thru the churning
history of an oppressed people—-your commanders
have not saved you from this slaughter-house
any better than the politicos,how many minds
moldered in distant confusion over how the Iraqis
have sacrificed everything to be anarchically free
as the crazed offspring of a still-hanging Father?

Before & since the surge into deadly Baghdad
each of you had the same chance to survive:

either intact,maimed or killed,since death
comes once at a time on days when patrolling
to save the populace from such baleful hatred
of their countrymen,since having more of you
in the capital does not spare all of you
day after night, & luck is never democratic
in the hands of the bloodily righteous. Who is able
to walk home still has the war in your chest,
it roars in your dreams & startles your heart
from noises & worries,your wives say you left
your specialness in Iraq & more of a walking corpse
lives here now,the worst of you kill yourselves
because the war is that most ungrateful mistress
demanding your civilian here-after. The wounded
struggle to gain strength & accept plastic limbs,
feel steel plates in your heads & to stop conjuring
the wish to be whole--how you sacrificed
graced us with the laziness not to complain
to Washington to save you from being sent at all,
we are the mildest Iraqis against our own brethren
since we no longer love soldiers protecting us
but send you off to battle & hungrily turn away,
no homecoming parade with 10,000 loyalists
for every veteran,as only the widows know better.

You amongst the other dead walking thruout
Heaven's crowded claim-space as the valiant
-ly fighting men crossing the blood-brick wall
to find God in this mystical fourth dimension
called Time-less Thriving,
                            4,000 saviours
at least of freeom if not the lives of others
who,at full moon,come into a ragged circle
to speak of all those left behind on Earth
as murmurs of mourning rise in Heaven
no less sufferable than here. Heaven ineffable
for us waiting to be received,is there peace
from losing comrades & the many families
to increately stroll over its grassy plentitude
counting your blessings--where is the blood
that is joy & weeping in this Saving Place
of constant virtues,there being no world
to save once God balms our foolishness
with the grace of forever?

47

                        In fire-fights
you knew the feel of crucifixional ambush
suspending your lives between warfare & death,
where to live is to be scarred & to carry on
        in the realm of trembling passage
     to another day of agony incarnate,
so which of you taps on the blood-brick wall
asking God to go back home or down to Iraq
to finish the work,to fight the zealots
to save our human truths? How long
has it taken for any of you to jerkily shout
         I don't want to stay here yet,
knowing that going home is not Godly possible
beyond a persuasive Jesus for lonely disciples
yearning for Him to Lordly stay.
                        Fill your circle
with some of the thousands of Iraqi civilians
also immured in this alembical Saving Place,
since Heaven must by now be the stretched size
of the history of our world,gravidly surpassing us.

            April 2-4, 2008

BEFORE THE POLITICAL

comes the personal,earlier than
cashed slogans & campaign tantrums
to change what of our world so bad
-ly thrives beyond us,what candidate
strokes our hearts & minds with the personal
to resonate change thru crowds at rallies
so long before we will next elect a president
once voters are counted as market share
in corporate politics,as New England scruffiness
dies after the first primaries—-the personal
abraded by cattle-trampage criss-crossing
too many states to even remember our faces
across the miles of chasing count-less votes
cashed to ambitiously win. Newspapers,
magazines & television sniff out any stories
worthy of skinnier print to proclaim victors
& strugglers ten months before the primaries
-cash raised in the millions,as tho gasoline
builds the car—-our nation daily blathers
its politics with the reckless condescension
of tattle-tailing about a drunken civics lesson
whose merit gets lost amidst our sloppily falling
to the floor,one & all smeared with the fetid
-ly menacing smell of rotten-spots on chances
to o'er-leap the feeble walking our politics
does on all other days.

                         Is it whether
gender or misericordia or cash at-hand
fingers the form of our votes,children
or where we live,what pricks us nearly
every day to mention such to certain others
called how plentiful our political brethren
up-raised beyond the wrath-rousing malaise
of democracy's idiot dopes. Some vowels of politics
once rhymed with *listen*,even to those foolish
-ly loose with the facts & wind-fully indignant,
so with twenty-five years of blistering schism
from Ronald Reagan to Karl Rove,the radio
shouting with all shades of virulent wisdom,

who truly knows how to plaster the holes
of our national soul? It is these & other
riving men who listen least, our president
—who pretends to listen but knows even less,
whose wisdom shivers in its daily infancy—
whom we must stand before to crawl under
your barbed rhetoric after having seen
              the world's sickly-plenty
to feed such salivating dog-men not more
gossip disguised as truth, but the prickly facts
of especially the war: since no American
can walk thru Baghdad unarmed after four years
of moldering Hell-fight, are we not united
in our ignorance of how to save a nation?

April 9-10, 2007

OUR LAST AMERICAN MANIFESTO

A win-grimaced Barack Obama as such rocky calmness hovering over our huge piles of smoking mortgages & rusting dreams, this mulatto'd skinny prince climbing the ladder of our prejudices for nearly two years to surely be crowned as a younger kingly persona coaxing our caution toward some alembical temperance called *the culled tonnage of our self-ruin,* our puerile spasms of debt forgotten until credit cards remember our names each month,what spells shall you cast to ease its weight enough that our backs can rest for even one day's worth to breathe any fresher air? How recession accepted you sooner than our prejudices could stomach the black aura of your countenance,your vagaries of hope for our lives said eight years of nothing have been the sodden arithmetic bushing our commerce into the swelling swamp of foreclosure & salvage-sales-—the colour of a saviour glimpsed but not begrudging you,since Jesus had a look unknown to our American faith in Him. Out of this clamantly pellucid election,shall we become any less immured in our hated of another's race—-unspoken as it has been from your mouth—-what of your work toward our national salvation shall God thru you render us humbler as to how slavery did not destroy what in blacks outlasted the whitest mutilation of your soulish prosperity,having sweated in old Southern fields,or shall it now be called the Half-Black House?

You have reminded us there are common causes in democracy's floundering wastage which need work & care,that we became one people earlier against the British & later the Nazis, but without such hatred of foreigners pestering us,we turn upon each other in blame & murder,since we are a violent people once our privileges get bothered,our middle names being borrowed from television & our customs are streaked with the cheap plastic of selfish manners. Remind our young ones of the names & purposes of these common causes,for they never knew of such muscular service to a country enriching them beyond slavery & the contagious penury of famine & disease-it is only this year they have come to feel any sense of poverty in at least their friends' bellys tho they can not yet spell charity as acts of self-less grace borne of your imploring the misericordia of strangers one to another that hurricanes foster in their terrorable malice, three years & counting. Who will build the bridges & tap the oil, what demands cars run only on gasoline, how does medicine coax cures from science fiction & how does a mulatto'd king-fisher troll for the American Soul in the debris of our trashy wealth? Americans still solve every problem at the last chance, we are still children bemoaning what dead grown-ups tried to foist upon us as that dreaded notion of responsibility: it is the stale licorice pulled from the attic that chokes our throats.

Food Stamps fed your belly for a while as a youngster, so you stare into the lives of the poor when sweating or shivering to find any up-rising wealth, such unkindly perditional hunger & life-lack dwelling in shacks & trailers on all sides of the local mountains, oodles of crops idle or sent to save the starving elsewhere, those who stop us asking for cash to buy a meal say America is no longer a blessed place to live, whether or not from their own foolishness, how much rocking in broken chairs on front porches while the rain torments the poor as the soggy bounty of what God offers, will you eat Thanksgiving dinner with such a family as a mulatto'd Santa Claus coming early to cheer these little ones with the warmth of your own past sadness? Handouts & "welfare states" as the dogma-grind of Republican politics, Jesus would never run the Department of Health & Human Services because His charity boiled in Godly personal work with the sinning poor & not from Washington's tower-palaces-—foreign aid the pricklish dollars sent on our behalf to struggling countries trying to farm & build schools, drink cleaner water & live peaceably better, those making fifty cents a day know the taste of coins in their mouths & how to take mud-baths, so bring a few of them to Congress to let our representatives grimace & fidget until the poor tell stories of such transcendent generosity the press can not quote all the whitest sponsors.

No end-less fence for you to move past to reach the mainland from Hawaii's lusher paradisal homestead to go to classy schools before work in the ghetto taught you about poverty's awful smallpox, foreigners longing to join our squeak-mirror'd circus because our jobs pay for more than breaded sustenance & insected water, our Lady welcoming all those who are squirming with the money'd desire for freedom's lure to tongue our American sky & be cash-heavy glad. Those who nightly crawl beneath the border fence into our southwestern desert to work to send money home to their families, what is illegal about heaping the wealth of the poor thru hard work with no usable English to court the rest of us, they living the cultural divide between love & rejection, swarming us in chattering numbers that the arousal of our prejudice is coaxed aloud in the back of our hearts as who offers what to whom, brown-skinned & grinning. How many millions of illegal aliens do the tough work Americans will not touch in farm-fields & restaurants, what trucks or buses large enough to haul them back to Mexico 10,000 in a load, who of honourable worth to stay here--should you learn Spanish before the recession stalls their entry into our sanctuary, should you stand atop the border fence & thru a bull-horn pronounce them use-less to us, you whose own family scraped by in poverty's unbrittle grip before ambition itched your feet to be handsomely emancipated.

You want our name to be spellable to the world again, America the lumbering, oafish & embarrassing spectacle of hyped press & bragging incompetence, our solipsistic grandeur & foolish neglect, how we love ourselves dearly in the face of starvation & genocide, America full of dim-bulbed mirrors smashed & replaced from dime stores, crack the last mirror & our original beauty can be grudgingly beheld. No president will ever be waterboarded, 14 seconds of terrorable drowning for practice or for zealots, who loves to have their sex talk wiretapped & played for horny soldiers on Armed Forces Radio--our government lying to its people for eight years about war & science, about corporate greed & oil drunk by caribou, birth control only for the elderly as the Bushian mantra of Do nothing to save our world hangs from the vowels of America for the world to mock & burn. Yet we are still truly loved in spite of ourselves as the staggering mammoth drunkenly crashing the world's party to proclaim ourselves back again from the grave--you too will make this claim on

Inauguration Day,the presidential oath of our right-full dominance that size does matter as our phallic thrusts into worldly intercourse so being skinnier than the shadow our recklessness has cast from the war,how will you show our flag,re-stitched & pressed,waving to other countries to sing our anthem with the words smiling on their lips?

You speak of our imperiled planet wheezing from smog & tons of carbon dioxide clogging the air over China & Eastern Europe beyond the glitzy skies of Los Angeles,fires & melting polar icecaps as the oceans shall rise to soak our beachfront property with fetid marine sludge,slides & films of Natural destruction send us into denial's likeliest diet of junk food & soda pop—-She always dwarfing our Natural imagination & too-pokey science,only in the desert does such doom-laden prophecy sing the vowels of its warning that we as man-gods can not breathe & drink wholly on our own. Hybrid cars & wind-power will help but not solve our oil-lust,splitting the atom takes longer than pollution's swarming ugliness to stop, & who will conserve what is so easily charged & pumped when cheaper than walking or working? Bushian science corrupted by Republican corporate meddling & childish denial,an ignorant man growing dumber, eight years wasted. Of all your many promises,it is as Natural saviour you would thrive the brightest,the lastly sanguine are we who hope She can be well-healed before this Natural cancer metastasizes beyond enough cure to redeem our own survival-—if indeed God has sent you to save us,without suffering the trial of crucifixion,can you bless us with the sanctity of the greenest relief,pulling us out of the brackish swamp of our techno-death?

November 10-11,13 & 17-19, 2008

WHAT EVERY TORTURE MEMO SAYS

Today, after the usual draining course
of days of sleep deprivation, you bring me
into this nauseously hot room where the air
damply clings to my chest as tho Africa
becomes a sprawling continent in my torso,
I again blindfolded & laid upon a stretch-bed
wondering when my suffering shall commence
until I feel little pricks of movement
all over my body as fire-ants bite & sting me
thru the sweat weighting me nakedly awake,
no sounds otherwise to balm me from no scratching
allowed in preparing the altars of my crucifixion—
this goes on for hours until I pass out
from the stifling heat & the itchy pain
of your wanting all I know to tell you,
with fire beneath my skin I am shrieking
to be relieved of the orders sparing my country.

Early the next morning, I am startled awake
by blaring heavy-metal chords pumping my heart
in the worst concert ever to be witnessed
blasting on for hours until my ear-drums
crave silence as the gentlest sex for a virgin
christening me—eventually the same song
is played over & over to hard-bend my name
into Chatterbox, spelling my terrorist dogma
with the plans & locales for our operations,
I immured in this roaring & lonely secrecy
my trainers reminded me would beg me to kiss
death's pleasurable wedding of bliss & travel,
since Heaven allows no thrashing guitars
but only the sweet sounds of Lordly paradise.

Already sweating before breakfast, I am
pain-fully stretched to lengthen my answers
to your end-less questions about our jihad
& targets where you would forget to look,
it takes less than one hour to send me
yelling to Allah that our cause is just

& our enemies deserve to die—-at the end
of the first hour,this big-breasted naked babe
comes in to suck my cock but she will not
deep-throat my jism,her ass prettier
than those at home & so American decadence
kindly riles me-—by the second hour,I say
what convulses me: *we are wrong to spray*
our evil upon such wealthily good people,
tho our world veils its beauty under terror.

A full day goes by before you hang me
by my arms from the ceiling all afternoon
while playing cute baroque music softer
than days ago,again I am stretched
to confess what knowledge could save us
from your televised benevolence in commercials
banned from our people,what does America
have to offer the world besides techno-wealth
& shrill democracy—-your Jesus knew such
terrible pain well into an earlier afternoon
before imploding & then ascending into Heaven,
    these days of perditional wastage
fill your middle name as the wily leader
of American redemption from our evil,
so when will you comfort me with such
a fresh presence on Allah's Sunday looming soon?

Annealed to what you have gifted much
farther than Islam promises me to weather,
you order your stooges to jolt me harder
than these teases in failing to be up-raised
    into confession's royal favour
    that honesty bravely confirms me
as clairovoyant to stellar feats of tragedy,
so sooner than prayers are whispered & answered
my crotch is shocked once I again refuse
to spill our plans into your greedy laps-
all the questions,the bugs,the loudest music
& hanging upright over the hours of clammy torment
ring me with the aura of my confidence,
mewling because I am still bruisingly human
but Americans will never break my bones
or choke me,since democracy says freedom

is never blithely price-less—-upturned voltage
& my howling quakes the walls to endure me
until my eyes lie no longer: *you shall not*

break me of my curse to cloyingly destroy you.

The next morning after a filling breakfast,
I am laid upside-down upon a long board
as my mouth & nose are covered with a cloth
before water is poured upon my gagging face
             to drown what smiles in me,
this the worst rumour heard in training camp
about the daedal American torture you ordered
behind locked doors far from snooping cameras,
how volunteers from the CIA lasted only 14 seconds
before screaming to be freed,
                       Jesus never drowned
during His ministry tho you lost His righteousness
so early in this fresh century, so off & on
today you water-board me as I fly Heavenward
longer & better than your stooges,since our hatred
of America is the tastiest meal we nibble upon
day after year,the World Trade Center in our bellys.

      *

On the seventh day,as when God rested
to gaze upon the bounty of His world
-ly Creation,I am spared another round
           of undyingly ripe torture
but am privileged to finally meet you
face-to-face in this ornery agony felt
while trying to sleep,
                   you do not scare me
with your balding,chubby countenance
spectacled & grinning with the man-god
's clever sense of bending time & tolerance
         toward how you maim your brethren
from hiding places with slick maneuvers
admired by our own malefic master-mind,
Osama bin Laden. You & I are much
the same: cherishing dogma,obdurate

-ly convincing to those who doubt you,
charmingly deceptive & truly certain
          of your unharmed righteousness,

you a worthy enemy for crazed terrorists
who love the world that must be our own
to crack & conquer. For a little while
we gently stare at one another, waiting
for the other to ask such needled questions
about dominance & the necessity of Law,
& about how women will rarely understand us
in our willingness to die for common cause,
but would you harness a womanly terrorist
lovelier than stretched death?
                              You know
there are thousands of us waiting to kill you
          as the face of American torture,
I know there is a days-long lecture
about democracy trembling behind your face,

but each of us knows the other will not listen
in this holier war to be victorious,
so before we can unmercifully tease each other,
I ask you this best question from beneath you:
          Dick Cheney, how shall prison suit you?

                    April 20-23, 2009

AN EARNED SERVANT SPEAKETH

I was more than half-strongly called
into Godly service once my age oldened
past my first bad job of unmerciful work
as a white-collared production manager
because my soul out-grew such business
of manufactured goods,how else finding
any real goodness than where better sprouted
         thru its working in churches,
causitry less hobbled here even on other days
as our Lord nudges those who still listen

to the awe-full suffering of Jesus Christ
before & after His ascension into Heaven—-
there is no other story that more puzzles our minds
yet pricks our hearts,Jesus daily nags at us
thru His unsimple gifts of besting generosity,
so find Him rousing you now. I can not
lend my calling to many of my parishioners,
it is barely teachable & the too-blind leap

's bottom terrifies anyone whose trust melts
from vexing hardship's muscular plunge,
confession good for the soul whose unconscious
well-follows you,but our faith always
"wrestles with Jesus every unwoken day"—-
we have become too scienced to let any man
-god's crucifixion pellucidly prove to us
that God fashions our likeness in His image
as the Father who royally offers. My sermons
snare your wakefulness to thru me let God
better prod your faith with His wisdom

while you sit & allow me to rouse you
toward His grace,the words bathed in His aura
once I have first been blessed to utter His Scripture
to seal Godly providence deeper between your ears

until your hearts have been again mild
-ly righted,my sermons the less wandering
compass of a righteous man with so much
to give on Sundays & thru the week's rain-
what else so well feeds us? What do you know
of the Bible's unruined truths,the leap of faith
is to read all of its verses & bravely surrender
to the alembical transcendence the New Testament
                blooms richer than springtime,
have you learned the twinings of this weathered text
to merely recite them,or to peel their thin flesh
to taste of the Lord's bounty? Beyond tempting sins
from the crass modern idolatry of pagan television
& the curvaceous sleek feel of sexual women
lies the thorn-bush of how we are to forgive

those who trespasses sting harder than
blood-bruises,when trust is water-logged
with pretenses & lies to gain our favour,
when criminals steal or maim any of us
in the unnecessary mischief of cheap evil;
whose heart is easily cleansed of taming rage
to sit in a jail cell with any man murderous
-ly disturbed,Jesus calling us to lay ourselves
aside from revenge-does forgiveness heal
we sinners,this is what some of you ask me
& I must honestly answer: *too scarcely rare
for Godly redemption.* Sins born & prospering
       in the stray-pit of the unconscious,

where Jesus' Resurrection is only the most curious
history-prize,since His life was not ours

& confession carries us forward only to the next
wrestlable temptation,how many eternal parents
can anyone have? Jesus never kissed & fondled
any of His admiring women & so was immortal
-ly chaste,what is God's love compared
to that of a beautiful woman,with whom
to sleep & pray thru the long wintertime,
how easily are we special ones to be forgiven?
I being one of those venerably groomed

to receive the celibate celebration of Heaven
's refulgent presence as the unclouded nirvana
of saints & bunglers--in yet another myth
it is said Heaven lies in the fourth dimension
filled with the risen dead proclaiming God

's impalpable talent for such Fatherly caresses,
   this lastingly answered prayer
cornered in the aether, let us be released
into such beseeching Godly arms.   So come
often to the House of the Lord to worship
to votively know the Scriptures bathe us
not in hollow promises but how faith breaks
the shackles of sin & any stranger wastage
to feel the sung vowels of rectitude & righteousness,

let me or any priest drip our holier water
upon your faces & place the cherished wafer
in your mouths to churn a burning variance
   for God in your souls yearning
to be bountifully saved--beyond oblations,
tithes & duties let any of we special ones
walk you down to the altar to be blessed
by He who claps as we assume His purpose.

April 12-15, 2005

THIS DAILY SOLILOQUY

No manly dreams as terrorable as this
Godly order to stake My wrists & ankles
to the Cross in sacrificial torment
for hours of heat-lit fortitude
demanded from whispering to Pontius Pilate:
I am Jesus, seize-such, the Son
     of our God who clots us from Heaven
's venerable soul-post,
                         clotting death
-ly crucifixion with sweating forgiveness
as you study Me for signs of beguiling Him
deeper into day-blood, slowly annealing Myself
to the sting-ache-heaves of sin-less living
to save you thru the end-less centuries of
malignantly shouting My name as the Saviour
from your bottom-less causes. Those who love Me
as well as those who scratch your soul-lessness
are gathered here at Golgotha to withstand
My suffering to knife your unconscious
for all generations, beholding Me in becoming

the bruised & bloody causitry of our goodness,

wretching upright for hours & thousands
of days as your prayers are poured upon Me
as the one Man alembically charged to save you
from the nadiring place of dead redemption––
I will hang here until the sun daily lives
In your bellys, & I will never nicely die.

          *

I was the star-shown baby born to His children
raised to not fulfill God's prophecy until
He told Mary I would come to whiten you,
     My mother whose faith swelled
          faster than rumours could crack you,

who traveled with & for Me wiser than those
who clamoured for zealous knife-thrusts
into the bellys of all our many oppressors—-
you & Joseph,My father,impalpably promised
to do our Lord's work within & beyond the Temple
once puberty strayed Me nowhere else,girls
& women came to me tho sinners of
both genders wailed the same. So soon I quoted
Scripture because I had to outgrow such tutelage
before My brother baptized Me in the river,
work & women for years but never against God
did I strive to utter My name as surpassing Him
            in wanton,cock'd idolatry,
I never married but tongued the Scriptures
among women,who know God from your own
blessed children—-do not ask Me how I lived
before the river-cure,*since it was all only
urging Myself forth to serve God's orders
that He be dyingly obeyed*.
                        My brother,
John the Baptist,ferally shouted to those
who yearned for the slaking of your thirst
            for God's holy river-rise,
he was head-spent for My sake & who but God
balms any smeary guilt,that one man should die
in quivering ardor of another at the whim
of a pretty dancing maiden,selfish Salome.

From the host of unrepeated hours & all
the eyes of God,I chose twelve disciples
to follow Me thru the heresies of men
's coarser dominion to tame your preferences
into one pruning posture: *to grow humbler
in the face of all our worldly prejudices*,
twelve men who fought Me harder than
Scripture portrays in your twitching & sleepy
            doubt about My transcendence,
tho who else would dissolve your lives
upon My calling,upon the whims of benevolence
whispered by God? I healed a few of the sick,
sighted others & vanquished one man's tremors
until,in raising Lazurus from the dead
after four days,you named Me the Messiah
& I cupped your mouth,Peter the wisest one,

to spread no tales of My talents beyond wishes
to be sparingly re-born. Turning another cheek
or meekly bowing before the strength to be
struck down for others,the field lilies & birds
sow no work nor splay fire from base deeds,
teaching all known to Me from God's bounty
to frailer Spirits on the long road to Jerusalem
where Scripture is gashed upon My holier flesh
more brutally than anything else ever granted
simply by being faith-full.
                           I forgive
those who are not thirsting to be righteous
-ly caressed by Me,who grows rectitudinal
-ly stronger with wisdom's mantic clarity,
even he who burdened Me with My Cross
hauled thru the streets to reach Skull-Stop
after My brethren surrendered Me to Pilate
in proclaiming nothing but God's awe-full truth:
            I am King of the Jews,
but tell no one unless his wrath has diluted
into the last conversation about the real Messiah
living amidst you after all. Do not truly ask
to be crucified,only I could be so blessed
in receiving this gift of ineffable pleasure,
if God abandons Me hanging this vertically,
sky to ground,with My chest imploding minute
upon hour as His annealing sacrifice of Me
to later save your souls,my disciples scattered
to be relieved of your head-split knowledge
                of witnessing the Son of God
                shackle-stung of mortals
surely Pilate shall cry while I hang dying
to be up-lifted into Heaven's soul-clouded glory,
tho watch Me no longer than your repentance
blooms a steadfast faith in torturous miracles,
since I must leave you to grind your history
into anguish with My Father daily cursing
your many transgressions,balefully love-sick.

      *

As I am always hanging,on at least
such certain days to memorably hover

              again in birth & death
over how you waveringly pray to be cleansed
or be granted such peace at My birth-time,
moved from springtime to winter to feel
          light in the pivoting winter
           lean from Me then back to Me
as you scurry to buy & wrap your presents
after knocking each other down at dawn
once the stores have roused you to save
more on what owns you, at Christmas
I am merely the babe who is gifted
& not yet the hanging man blackening Friday
with My bloody Wastage. Sales in My name
bless cash registers & the evening news says
        this is your well-earned goodness
bathing the economy with the water of your greed
       once God is never necessary
for you to sit around the greenest tree thanking
each other for not being awkwardly forgotten
with the bad gifts re-opened year after year,
having prayed to be so pleased. You are hope-less
-ly smitten with the crookedly palest gold,
frankincense & myrrh, so bring your tithes
of 10% of all you earn & pour it into the river,
flooding Her with the coinage of your lives
where it clinks no more, tho My groaning
is drowned out by these gifts from Judas Iscariot.

I hang here awaiting Heaven's ever-lasting lesson of sufferable usurpage of your uglier human past-times of deceit & warfare, your vicious ignorance of the Holy borne upon Me until I nearly collapsed in the square while you watched & whispered about My failing to save Myself, Heaven being no abstract wish for the righteously redeemed, having prayed for years to taste its remedying nectar. God has hinted to me that Heaven lies in the fourth dimension outside of our lives to allow for homes for all the deserving dead souls from long ago, as large as a galaxy, whose passage comes at death or when we slip into the unconscious white light for those blessed moments between life & death, before being slammed back alive-any doubt about God then vanishes, & to explain this to others is the same as My own miracles, how do you describe the world to the blind or deaf? Heaven is My reason for hanging aloft for all of your many skins,if you could see My resurrection it would wind up on television as the blasphemy of the divine, so let its miraculous soul-thrust-upward taunt your mortality to bend you into God's worthier servants for longer than your envious prayers.

        *   *

If Heaven is My worthiest respite
after this barely sufferable work
of saving you from all your plagues,
you always soon forget Me afterward
once I ascend to live with My Father
because your children lose sight of parents
in a crowd gathered to laugh or be healed--
the crosses around your necks prodding
what in you could mercifully serve others
& not merely adorn your swarmy beauty,
since God ages us not in taut wisdom
but in wrinkled regrets. I must hang
& not up-raise Myself into Godly favour,
My crucifixion must last each of your lifetimes
to abrade the tinslish commerce of gifts
of Devil-prone gravity,
                                  it is My agony
that jerks your faces toward the sky
& the churches to somehow be relieved of
this squeamish blood-rust from your lives
wiped upon the pews before the offering
of what else you have so easily earned
clinking into the plate.
                          I am exhausted
from the friction of your strengthening Me
    the length of your soul-less
-ly rejecting Me after Pilate & the Sanhedrin,
my own family & you disciples until after
I returned to you in the Upper Room,
you later died for Me after I proved
My resurrection was not a liar's tale—-
all the rest of you whose middle name is
Thomas,bore your forefingers into the gash

in My side,while asking: *why does My story
last forever,You can never forsake Me
because the proof of Me is My Father's world.*

December 4,6,8,11-12,15 & 18, 2006

THIS YULETIDE'S TONGUE SPEAKING FREELY

We heard all the sky-gracing stories
before Jesus was born,all the heroic
& vain-struck gods & goddesses beheld
to shrink our human purpose beneath
their unseen royalty,the Egyptians & Greeks
long before the divine portrayals of miracles
of healing & the up-risen dead startling
all those curious about our humble man-god,
stories of sky-drenched warfare & love
reddening the heavens as life-lit melodrama
weighting our people with their purpler courage
& popular penance drawn from looking skyward
with our pallid mortality. The Garden of Eden
was earth-bound & clear-heartedly human,
temptation & sin before the Flood cleansed us
& the lineage of David walked toward where
His birth would grow unrivaled in our lore:
a baby born at winter's solstice in a stable,
confounding those for whom all earlier stories
melted & fizzled upon seeing Jesus' first glory-
found in churches,shopping malls & on television
only half-less miraculous even this late
in our own reckless century,
                              the swallowing story
seeably true thru the barbarism at Golgotha,
two thousand years & still ungangreenous
-ly true, we fidget before the Nativity
as the scene of our eye-cocked redemption,
chipped but not cracked apart by so much debt.

We read the symbols & the disobeyance
against God as how our faith should dwell
in our hearts & deeds to glorify His name
on each exhalation before falling asleep
to savour our service as charitably necessary
to relieve our world of some of its sloth
& to allow repentance to manifest itself
thru soulish work in the lives of others—
Christianity a lantern in the darkness
of the cave of human sin to alight salvation

& bring joy to those pagans unrighteous
-ly denied the bounty of Lordly goodness
Jesus died to provide us. We read the Bible
as the stories of our struggles to be freed
of our vices to be rendered humbler before others,
              since God always watches us
            as even His worst servants
-the Creation offered for our ascension
into a moral benevolence daily offered in thanks
for such worldly bounty, knowing our world
without God's love is too rarely truly enough,
owing everything we are, we have & we do
to His glory, Mecca for Christians being
where our last goodness overwhelmed someone
& they also prayed aloud. Even if thickly invisible,
God show Himself thru end-less Natural examples
& circumstantial grace, He is not hiding, crying
over our mistakes & our malice, altho we do
wonder how God spend His time awaiting
our still-rumour'd transcendence, recalling
it has been thirty years since a songster
from Liverpool was so admiringly murdered.

The Old Testament stories are human
-ly skewed to pull our purpose inside us,
tho would not happen so easily otherwise
in feeling stung by the heat of burning bushes,
so God birthed Jesus in the manger to common
-ly call us back to how we grow righteous
from His alembical stance of obvious prophecy:
healing the sick & raising the dead before
His own Heavenly resurrection,
                           The New Testament
shorter yet riper from one vatic man-god
bleeding to be believed. All atheists are disappointed
with God & long to be visited at night by Jesus
to balm their wounds, it is their childish denial
of how what can not be seen can not be believed
unless Jesus returns to fulfill anyone's longing
to be christened as finally saved. Atheism
says God never made the world or we do not
need Him anymore, that we are self-sufficient
& religion is an overdose of dogmatic bludgeoning,
Karl Marx ranting on cable television

in a funny hat & suspenders. God not found
in most churches,He floats over the roofs
& prays we look Heavenward for His Son's face
in the shape of ordinary sky,so how is Christianity
clearly special? Going to church in America
is to be thrown only the occasional strike
amongst too many balls & intentional walks
from clergy struggling to hit the strike zone
by hurling fastballs dizzy with theological meaning,
        turning our heads in devout attention
to these men who survived the seminaries
to become holier than staying home. Church
can be about finding the empty tomb every Sunday
until God rattles what happens to bend Himself
into pellucid beauty,His relevance tasting
better than only chewing on pages from the Bible
& capiciously wishing. Everything we read
becomes the collapsing history allowing faith
to blossom once we are graced with the truth we know,
there being no atheism in deathly white light.

    *

Our faces sometimes sniffing for the sight
of You amidst Her bounty as the Creator
of Natural awe impalpably caressing us
without the politics of muddy compromises
or deathly transgressions killing our chances
        for humilitous redemption,
our unconscious poking thru the woods
in wintertime & all the mistakes we regret
        for signs of the face
        of our Father knowing us
from somewhere untouchable thru the years
of our beseeching You,
        our faces turning
from signs of Your face upon whom prayers
need be placed with less blur-brained wavering
or twitching distemper,not merely mouthing
Your Son's prayer because we are drones
but wishing to be kissed by Your abrading presence
as midnight creaks & groans. We Christians
ignore You less than always & more than

our desire for Father-love,You our Father
of still-ineffable blessings, our prayers
wobbling or chirping to say what relieves us
to reveal what in anyway crests us toward
   souls swimming in Your righteousness,
since prayer drains atheism's fear to leap
into Your lap to be soothed,bathed & amazed.

The Bible's story is the supra-natural plea
to daily pray,if not unceasingly then
once the urge gurgles in our ruddy mouths
to say to You: *Do something grace-fully*
better with our hoary world,
      cheaply ease
our worries or our sadness quicker than
the pain-full hours of Your Son's crucifixion,
we being impatient & Your time moves slower
than our pokey devotion.
     Prayer stumbles
our leap into Your lap,tho it bumbles us
homeward as our necessary apprenticeship
over dreaded spans of time swaying our unconscious
   You are at all worthy of us,
such has been our nadiring patronage of You
since Adam & Eve. Sin is our favourite reason
for even talking to You,being so easily forgiven
by the clergy in the Reassurance of Pardon,
to "Go & sin no more" might nauseate Jesus
if He were not divine,we only rarely mewling
 unto You as the Master upon whom
 we more than ephemerally depend
—what pretty woman would seduce her priest
with the antics of her wanton adultery,
her words full of the cleavage beckoning him?

Strolling thru the doughy ambage that is
our Christian faith,
     returning to prayer
to garner the robes of servile humility
before You,once our beloved techno-salvation
leaves us asking: *What can we not do ourselves*
   to right our long-suffering world,
how often I forget You are hovering somewhere

over us as tho Creation outlasts even You
-call it *surrender* to He who must stay
unseen yet Master-full, blatantly more
than the hollower proclamations atheism makes
to center ourselves amidst this vast universe
's life elsewhere being still conjectural?
                      So,nightly,
already prone to the sky,some of nothing
firmer than rote blather smally graces my lips:

Take what never surrenders in me to coat
my body with the salve of Your countenance
to hasten the tiny deaths of my audacious
-ly writhing unconscious—forty years after
my own father's death—gaining Your face
thru the blinder strokes of emptying myself
when nothing comes but rasping chatter
-how to grow a church in my belly,
not only with Bible stories but to strain
the wisdom from all the many centuries
thru what must happen,the world & I,
You served with my grateful plain-tongue
to do Your worldly work sooner than never.

                              December 7-10 & 14-15, 2010

BANISH US OUTWARD

What released from whose uncrowded mind
less richly than anyone's curdled blather
coughed thru the telephone's othered illness
as how I grow malcontented from nurturing
a bothersome woman who thirstily faints
before your own more organic selfhood,
I having heard about everyone's lasting damage
yet what sits before me is too rarely lovable
beyond breaded mercy,where your flame
dimmed to wishes & the singing of flat
-tened stanzas half-remembered & hoarsely so,
take no fresher care of me but do nurse yourself
back to any malady's disclaimer. Never
enough of the death-spelled news about drugs
abused in the violent cacophony of your heart
's bending its weather to be stupidly soothed,
      this worstly medicinal candy
bought,sold & used because our world haunts
too many to place the grave-stones upon your heads
while wheezing to breathe,such a perfect bubble
cracked by heaving vomit,diarrhea & your noses
running a daily marathon—-surely your best news
being the poppies in Afghanistan may not grow
so plentifully this year,what farmer's conscience
louder than forageable piles of shinier coins
glinting of the sun's bounty. Not only chimes
resounding on a warm wintertime afternoon
but where the sky traces white sprawls of cloud
-y scripture whose causitry cruelly alludes us
until the stars offer a prick-thin synopsis
        of Naturally awesome knowledge
ignorant of our papery travails of softest calculus
called exponentially exploding heart-ache,
drape cow-bells around our necks to be found
closer to the path before our love becomes
wobbly then disasterous,all the waves
before & during the mistakes of such beloveds
whose risk tumbles & plunges. Fingering even
any branch attached to love's whirl-spin
cracks our solipsistic scorn for the one-eyed
tantrums of loneliest pox & to be so relieved

is riper than mere mouthing about a cure for
our babbling angst,come stroke any part of me
as the best remedy for our modern hygiene
's plastic'd uppity eye-jerks to beset you
with the urban rejection of human comfort—-
              how I can never settle into you
sooner than ringed marriage,no firm branches
grabbed earlier than talk of how the altar
heals the mischief as the worst of our foolish youth,
there being no digestible science in how love
itches us all over day after year,no real party
but its ragged bust-ups frazzle the kids
until they later fashion its surer trajectory
in their own half-piloted lives. Who argues
with anyone whose tongue pecks on our ears
in shrill laments about lapsing happiness,
how does misery gain solace thru complaints
juicier than writhing silence,find the sun
in the stormy sky as the white-lit compass
palmable in our lifetimes,when is sex better
than amidst buttressing love,how to pull you
to me against the dryness & prickly mishaps
love courts in living itself,love crucifixional
in its bloody death & congested resurrection,
love upon money not the advertised contest
but wrestled down faster than chance's slim bet.
Those forsaken by love squat in the hollowness
of sincerest wishes unrequited & lacerated
by bad chemistry,psychic strife & diseases,
increately clouded sun & tears between rains
upraises the dateable ones in abstentia knocking
not upon hearts lost to newly touchable love,
where to be huggably found? What is found
are other fond hobbies of strident life & pride
in being alive: do see & smell what becomes us,
even lambent examples of coloured scenes
particular to a day's suddenly bent resonance
unquestionably felt as the wet transcendence
                of how life properly walks

-having stumbled & skipped thru the river
long after birth nudged us to unwind ourselves
to be well-stretched before blur-dated death,
mother & father released in testable waves

of anxious passage to stand taller than thumb
'd stories of marvelous grow-up, *what is all
mine hereafter* in our bodily pockets unmined
or distilling into blessed success. How does everything
become minded taffy for we who stopped working
with our hands to spare ourselves stommy-lack,
no other mammals this dumbly so, our late century
's warpage coats all that is brought before us
as even verse is contorted to box the wattage
of our estranged play-time: a tune-fisted
new song of decaying waywardness, how well-sung

even in abstracter patterns of hollower promises
of telling you I will somehow o'er-leap myself
purposed to well-keep you, such poorly floating
dirigibles of plainest failures, I madly scamper
thruout a round box & call it bitterly important
as the next discovery will be out-held to you
in my mustably righteous hands. Too timid
are such promises once strutted & preened
to appease you, my soul-lessness flagrant
-ly tripping over all I have ever vowed to you,

what in me wanders farther than reason
's rarely fingered oracular penance, I spell
-ing love as drooping vowels in wire mesh,
no cage but leaking promises to be plugged
with frantic talk-caulk, how I bend myself
to wisely ill-suit you, never schizophrenic
but my oddness can clobber you. No tale
well-told to one bruisedly wronged, what truth
  smellable with easy distinction
from no con artist but how my mind caught
its worsening fancy
      to stay plainly straight
to harvest more than omens to lock me down
  upon love's looming truth––
I washed your heart with scraps of my ambition
& uncurved servitude, I felt marriage
  overwhelm my uncommon name
in my betrothal to wed me to your heart's care,
what collapsed was the normalcy of conveniences
as my mind spilt itself

                  upon the world's crust
& destroyed it—-no blame for your departure
because my rottenness would never spare you
-this we both know—-I no basking pageantry
          of untrampeled god's-call.

                 February 7-11, 2005

ABOUT THE AUTHOR

Marc Williams has been writing poetry since 1978, & also composes classical music for chamber & vocal ensembles. He has been a practicing psychotherapist since 1980, & lives in North Carolina. *Our Grieving Eden* is his first book of poetry.

Made in the USA
Charleston, SC
08 October 2011